# 101 FAMILY JOKES

# Make Me Laugh!
# 101 FAMILY JOKES

by Sam Schultz / pictures by Joan Hanson

Copyright © 1982 by Lerner Publications Company

All rights reserved. International copyright secured.
No part of this book may be reproduced in any form whatsoever
without permission in writing from the publisher except for
the inclusion of brief quotations in an acknowledged review.

Library of Congress Cataloging in Publication Data

Schultz, Sam
  101 family jokes.

  (Make me laugh)
  Summary: A collection of 101 jokes about families
and family relationships.
  1. Family — Anecdotes, facetiae, satire, etc.
2. Wit and humor, Juvenile. [1. Family-Anecdotes,
facetiae, satire, etc. 2. Jokes. 3. Riddles]
I. Hanson, Joan, ill. II. Title. III. Title: One
hundred one family jokes. IV. Title: One hundred and
one family jokes. V. Series.
PN6231.F3S34      818'.5402       81-20861
ISBN 0-8225-0981-4                AACR2

Manufactured in the United States of America

        5  6  7  8  9  10  91

**Mary:** We've got a new baby at our house.
**Terry:** Is he going to stay?
**Mary:** I guess so. He brought all his clothes.

**Willie:** Dad, can I have a dollar so I can go see Joey next door?

**Dad:** Why do you need a dollar to go see Joey?

**Willie:** Because his mother said he was at the movies!

**Father:** Why did you put that frog in your sister's bed?

**Eddie:** Because I couldn't find any worms!

**Q:** What do you call your mother's father when he's good to you?

**A:** A Grand-father.

**Alfie:** Dad, there's a small PTA meeting tomorrow that you have to come to.

**Dad:** If it's a small one, do I have to go?

**Alfie:** Yes, you have to go. It's just you, me, and my teacher.

**Mother:** Debby, I thought I told you to put salt in the salt shaker.
**Debby:** I tried, Mom, but I couldn't get the salt through all those little holes!

**Mother:** Chuck, be careful with that hammer. You might hit your fingers.
**Chuck:** No I won't, Mother. Johnny's going to hold the nails.

**Q:** What always stays hot in the refrigerator?
**A:** Horseradish.

**Johnny:** Will you marry me?
**Betsy:** You'll have to ask my father first.
**Johnny:** (later) Well, I asked him.
**Betsy:** And what did he say?
**Johnny:** He said he's already married.

**Father:** Cindy, have you seen the newspaper?
**Cindy:** Yes, Mother wrapped the garbage in it and threw it out.
**Father:** Darn. I'd like to have seen what was in it before she threw it out.
**Cindy:** I can tell you what was in it, Daddy. Some chicken bones, coffee grounds, and old vegetables!

**Mother:** Would you like me to give you something for your cold?
**Child:** Yeah, how about a quarter?

**Father:** Son, I've got a surprise for you. You've got a new baby sister!
**Son:** Oh! Does Mommy know about the surprise yet?

**Voice over Phone:** Is your mother home?
**Little Girl:** Yes, she is.
**Voice:** Will you call her to the phone, please?
**Little Girl:** Okay, but I'll have to go down the street to get her.
**Voice:** I thought you said she was home!
**Little Girl:** She is. This is my friend's house. I live down the street!

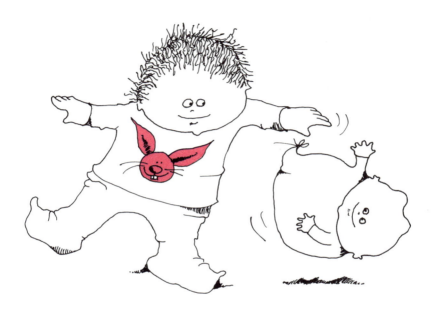

**Mother:** Willie! How did the baby get all these bumps on his head?
**Willie:** Well, you said he was a bouncing baby boy. But I couldn't get him to bounce!

**Sally:** Does your mother tuck you in every night?
**Wally:** No, she plugs me in. I have an electric blanket!

**Mother:** Jackie! It's after dark. You should have been home an hour ago.
**Jackie:** Why? What happened?

**Teddy:** Dad, can I please have a dime?
**Dad:** I think it's time you stopped asking me for dimes.
**Teddy:** Okay, how about a dollar?

**Mother:** Eat your green beans, Sonny. They'll put color in your cheeks.
**Sonny:** Who wants green cheeks?

**Ann:** Our house is going to be warm this winter.
**Pam:** How do you know?
**Ann:** My father just painted it and he gave it two coats.

**Q:** What's a good time to go to the dentist?
**A:** Tooth-hurty (2:30).

**Ann:** Do you have a grandfather?
**Jan:** No, but he's okay.

**Visitor:** Can you play on the piano, Judy?
**Judy:** No, my mother won't let me climb up there.

**Don:** My father's a sound sleeper.
**Ron:** How do you know?
**Don:** His snoring wakes me up.

**Dick:** My father takes his hat off to only one person.
**Rick:** Who's that?
**Dick:** His barber.

**Aunt:** Would you like to teach your new baby brother how to talk, Susie?
**Susie:** No, I'd like to teach him how to be quiet.

**Mother:** Bobby, there were 16 cookies in the cookie jar. Now there are only two. How do you explain that?
**Bobby:** I don't know, Mom. I thought I had gotten them all!

**Mother:** How many times have I told you not to come home late for dinner?
**Son:** I didn't know I was supposed to keep score.


**Gert:** My mother can make people do anything she wants them to.
**Bert:** Really? How does she do it?
**Gert:** She's a hypnotist!


**Q:** Why was the boy called Sonny?
**A:** Because he was so bright.


**Susie:** May I try on that dress in the window?
**Salesperson:** I'm sorry, ma'am, you'll have to do it in the dressing room!

**Q:** What should you take off before going to bed?

**A:** Your feet from the floor.

**Hy:** I have to go to the store to buy my mother some toothpaste.

**Sy:** Why, are her teeth loose?

**Q:** What do you call a dead parrot?

**A:** A polygon.

**Mother:** Here, Peter, this dust brush will do half your work for you.

**Peter:** Great! Give me two of them.

**Q:** Why are baby girls dressed in pink and baby boys dressed in blue?

**A:** Because they can't dress themselves.

**First Boy:** My brother won't give me *anything* of his.
**Second Boy:** Neither will mine. The only thing he ever gave me was chicken pox!

**Mother:** Tony, why is your little brother crying?
**Tony:** Because I won't give him any of my candy.
**Mother:** But I gave both of you candy.
   Has his been eaten already?
**Tony:** Yes, and he cried all the time I was eating it.

**Billie:** My pop can hold up a car with one hand.
**Willie:** Is he a weight lifter?
**Billie:** No, he's a traffic cop!

**Q:** What parent allows the kids to go to bed with their shoes on?
**A:** A horse.

**Mother:** Your cough sounds much better this morning, Barbie.
**Barbie:** It should. I've been practicing all night!

**There was a young lad** who said, "Why
Can't I have one more piece of your pie?"
His mother said, "Pet,
You ate all you will get."
So the lad could do nothing but cry.

**Mother:** Dotty! I told you to watch when the soup boils!

**Dotty:** I did, Mother. It boiled at exactly 6:15!

**Johnny:** My father bought my mother a new spring outfit.

**Tammy:** Really? What did he buy her?

**Johnny:** A rake, fertilizer, and some vegetable seeds.

**Mother:** Wendy, please come into the kitchen and help me fix dinner.

**Wendy:** Why, is it broken?

**Arnie:** Mommy, Daddy just fell off the 25-foot ladder!

**Mother:** Gracious, is he hurt?

**Arnie:** No, he just fell off the first step.

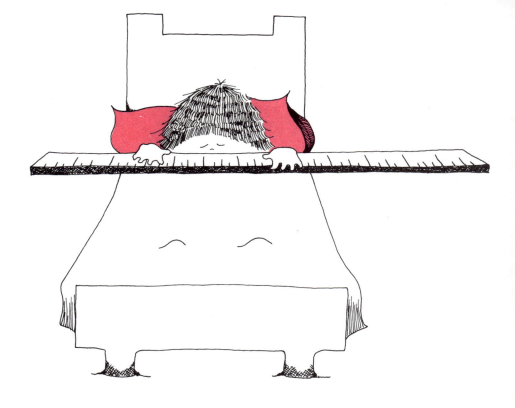

**Q:** Why did Billy take a ruler to bed with him?
**A:** To see how long he slept!

**Uncle:** Alice, I hear you went to the dentist today. Were you brave?
**Alice:** Yes!
**Uncle:** Well, for being brave, here's a dollar. Now tell me, what did the dentist do?
**Alice:** He pulled out one of my brother's teeth!

**Mother:** Jimmy, I thought I asked you to tell Billy that he could come here after supper.
**Jimmy:** That's what he's here after, Mom.

**Jack:** What makes you think your mother's trying to get rid of you?
**Mack:** Because she wraps my school lunch in a road map.

**Young Man:** I've come to ask for your daughter's hand in marriage.
**Girl's Father:** You've got to take all of her or it's no deal.

**Tillie:** (At restaurant) Mom, I can't eat this hamburger. It tastes awful!
**Mother:** Do you want me to call the waiter?
**Tillie:** No, I don't think he'll be able to eat it, either.

**Jimmy:** What have you got in that bag?
**Timmy:** Oats. It's a birthday present for my uncle.
**Jimmy:** Why oats?
**Timmy:** Because my mother says he eats like a horse!

**Betty:** My sister caught her boyfriend flirting.
**Jenny:** That's how my sister caught her boyfriend, too.

**Danny:** My father's studying to be an astronaut.
**Manny:** That a fact?
**Danny:** Yep. His boss called my mother and told her Pop was taking up space!

**First Camper:** I sure do miss my pet goldfish.
**Second Camper:** Why don't you drop him a line?

**Mother:** My goodness, Jerry, who gave you that black eye?
**Jerry:** No one gave it to me. I had to fight for it!

**Sandy:** Mom, is Dad still a growing boy?
**Mom:** No, why do you ask?
**Sandy:** Because his head is growing up through his hair.

**Mother:** Alice, tomorrow we're going to the doctor to have your eyes checked.
**Alice:** But Mom, you know I like polka dots better than checks!

**Annie:** Mother, the piano tuner is here.
**Mother:** Who sent for the piano tuner?
**Annie:** The neighbors!

**Dad:** If you study hard, son, you'll get ahead.
**Son:** But Dad, I already have a head.

**Ike:** I beat my brother up every morning.
**Mike:** Really?
**Ike:** Yep, I get up at seven, and he gets up at eight.

**Phil:** My dad shaves at least a dozen times a day.
**Ronnie:** How come?
**Phil:** He's a barber.

**Charlie:** What are you giving your mom and dad for Christmas?
**Artie:** A list of everything I want.

**Son:** Dad, why are you spanking me? I admitted I chopped down the cherry tree. Even George Washington's father didn't spank him for that.
**Father:** Yes, but his father wasn't *in* the tree when it happened!

**Q:** What's the best way to make anti-freeze?
**A:** Take away her electric blanket!

**Mother:** Charles, why are you standing in front of that mirror with your eyes closed?
**Charles:** I want to see what I look like when I'm asleep!

**Ellen:** Our scout troop is going on a 10-mile hike!
**Dad:** When I was your age, I thought nothing of walking 10 miles.
**Ellen:** I don't think much of it, either.

**Mother:** Billy, why is it that you get into more trouble than anyone else in the family?
**Billy:** I guess it's because I get up first.

**Mae:** My baby brother was born in a hospital.
**Fay:** Why? Was he sick?

**Mother:** Georgie, will you please take this pot of soup across the street to the Smiths, and find out how old Mrs. Smith is?
**Georgie:** (Returning) Mrs. Smith said it's none of your business how old she is!

**Mother:** Junior, why did you put mud in your sister's mouth?
**Junior:** Because it was open!

**Mother:** How did you get that hole in your new trousers?

**Jeff:** I fell off the swings.

**Mother:** Why did you do that in your new trousers?

**Jeff:** I didn't have time to take them off!


**Mom:** It's going to hurt me to punish you, son.

**Son:** Then don't do it, Mom. I don't want you to hurt yourself.


**Julie:** I'm writing a letter to my dog Fido.

**Jill:** But you don't know how to write.

**Julie:** That's okay. Fido doesn't know how to read!


**Q:** Why did Junior put ice in his father's bed?

**A:** Because he wanted a cold pop.

**Daddy:** Where did you get those beautiful eyes?
**Daughter:** Oh, they came with the face.

**Marty:** Mom, baby sister just swallowed my pencil.
**Mom:** My goodness, we've got to do something about that.
**Marty:** No, it's okay, Mom. I've got other pencils.

**There once was a girl** named Flack
Who lost her best dolly named Jack.
"Don't cry," said her mother,
"I'll buy you another."
Said Flack, "No, I just want Jack back!"

**Q:** What would you call your brother if he was
afraid to swim in the ocean?
**A:** Chicken of the Sea.

**Mary:** My father's a light sleeper.
**Harry:** Not my father. He sleeps in the dark.

**Molly:** My mother cooked for 100 people
yesterday.
**Polly:** What was the occasion?
**Molly:** No occasion. She works in a restaurant.

**Ned:** My brother sleeps on the bedroom chandelier.
**Fred:** Why?
**Ned:** Because he's a light sleeper!

**Danny:** Mother! The dog next door just bit off my toe.
**Mother:** You can't come in the house now, Danny. I just washed the floor.

**Tillie:** Why are you looking so sad?
**Millie:** We're supposed to go on vacation tomorrow, but my mother always gets sick the night before we leave.
**Tillie:** Then why don't you leave a day early?

**Salesman:** Will these stairs take me up to your house?
**Little Boy:** No, you have to climb them.

**Father:** Patty, would you like to join me in a bowl of soup?
**Patty:** Do you think there'd be room for the two of us?

**Mother:** Denny, how did you get your pants so wet?
**Denny:** I just washed them.
**Mother:** But why didn't you let them dry before you put them on?
**Denny:** Because the label says, "Wash and Wear!"

**Father:** Son, when you grow up I want you to be a gentleman.
**Son:** But I don't want to be a gentleman. I want to be just like you!

**Delivery Man:** Young man, is your mother home?
**Young Man:** Do you think I'd be pulling these weeds if she wasn't?

**Ginny:** We drove by your house yesterday and saw your family wash in the backyard.
**Winnie:** That's impossible. We wash in the bathroom!

**Mother:** Mickey, I can't hear you saying your prayers.
**Mickey:** That's because I'm not talking to you.

**Marty:** Mother, I just got Billy to stop biting his nails!
**Mother:** How did you do that?
**Marty:** I knocked his teeth out!

**Mother:** Joey, why did I catch you with your hand in the cookie jar?
**Joey:** Because I didn't hear you coming!

**Ellie:** When my mother's down in the dumps she always gets a new dress.
**Nellie:** I *thought* that's where she got them.

**Mother:** Tommy, go wash your face or Auntie Grace won't kiss you when she comes.
**Tommy:** Then I'd just as soon not wash, Mom.

**Mother:** Louie, I hope you didn't take two pieces of cake at Sally's birthday party.
**Louie:** No, I didn't Mom. I took three pieces!

**Grandmother:** The stork just brought you a little baby sister! Would you like to see her?
**Katie:** Well, okay. But I'd rather see the stork!

**Auntie:** Peggy, what would you want to do when you get to be as big as me?
**Peggy:** Diet.

**Mother:** You can't leave this house until you finish your alphabet soup.
**Daughter:** Honest, Mom, I can't eat another word.

**Bessy:** My brother has three feet.
**Tessy:** How do you know?
**Bessy:** He wrote my mother from college that he grew another foot.

**Q:** Why did the little boy's mother make him go to his bed?
**A:** Because the bed couldn't come to him!

## ABOUT THE AUTHOR

SAM SCHULTZ began telling jokes to children when his own were very young, and today he likes to think up new jokes while jogging on the beach near his home in Santa Monica, California. Mr. Schultz has been a writer for several advertising agencies, and now he writes scripts for television shows and children's films. He has also written plays, books, and songs. At the University of Southern California, Schultz majored in cinema and creative writing, with an emphasis on humor.

## ABOUT THE ARTIST

JOAN HANSON lives with her husband and two sons in Afton, Minnesota. Her distinctive, deliberately whimsical pen-and-ink drawings have illustrated more than 30 children's books. Hanson is also an accomplished weaver. A graduate of Carleton College, Hanson enjoys tennis, skiing, sailing, reading, traveling, and walking in the woods surrounding her home.

ELEPHANTS NEVER FORGET!
FACE THE MUSIC!
FOSSIL FOLLIES!
GO HOG WILD!
GOING BUGGY!
GRIN AND BEAR IT!
HAIL TO THE CHIEF!
IN THE DOGHOUSE!
KISS A FROG!
LET'S CELEBRATE!
OUT TO LUNCH!
OUT TO PASTURE!
SNAKES ALIVE!
SOMETHING'S FISHY!
SPACE OUT!
STICK OUT YOUR TONGUE!
WHAT A HAM!
WHAT'S YOUR NAME?
WHAT'S YOUR NAME, AGAIN?
101 ANIMAL JOKES
101 FAMILY JOKES
101 KNOCK-KNOCK JOKES
101 MONSTER JOKES
101 SCHOOL JOKES
101 SPORTS JOKES

Make Me Laugh!

CAN YOU MATCH THIS?
CAT'S OUT OF THE BAG!
CLOWNING AROUND!
DUMB CLUCKS!